TAMING CHAOS
WORKBOOK

"*Taming CHAOS* is an excellent and appealing way for students and families to learn about risk and making good decisions."

Sonia Levitin, *Award Winning,* German American Novelist, Young Adult Author and Holocaust Survivor

"Gary Miller's analysis of risk management is spot on. The book was written for teens, but it may interest college students too!"

M. Moshe Porat, Ph.D., CPCU, Dean, Fox School of Business, Temple University

"Adolescence is the frontier during which children transition from dreamers to doers. Unlike adults; however, teens do not have the brain development necessary to create and stick to concrete decisions in their best interest. *Taming CHAOS* provides young adult readers with a prescriptive decision-making tool that is woven into the fabric of this delightful novel about decision-making and managing risk to adopt a rescued dog. *Taming CHAOS*: charming, age-appropriate, relevant for young teens who struggle with decision-making at the onset of carving out their unique path in life."

Jeannie Hofmann, English Teacher, *Teacher of the Year,* Upper Moreland High School, Montgomery County, PA

TAMING CHAOS
WORKBOOK
Leaders Discussion Guide

GARY R. MILLER

New York

TAMING CHAOS WORKBOOK
Leaders Discussion Guide

Published in New York, New York, by Morgan James Publishing. Morgan James and The Entrepreneurial Publisher are trademarks of Morgan James, LLC.
www.MorganJamesPublishing.com

The Morgan James Speakers Group can bring authors to your live event. For more information or to book an event visit The Morgan James Speakers Group at www.TheMorganJamesSpeakersGroup.com.

Shelfie

A **free** eBook edition is available
with the purchase of this print book.

CLEARLY PRINT YOUR NAME ABOVE IN UPPER CASE

Instructions to claim your free eBook edition:
1. Download the Shelfie app for Android or iOS
2. Write your name in **UPPER CASE** above
3. Use the Shelfie app to submit a photo
4. Download your eBook to any device

ISBN 978-1-68350-155-8 paperback
ISBN 978-1-68350-156-5 eBook
ISBN 978-1-68350-157-2 hardcover
Library of Congress Control Number:
2016911397

Cover Design by:
Rachel Lopez
www.r2cdesign.com

Interior Design by:
Bonnie Bushman
The Whole Caboodle Graphic Design

I would like to thank those that supported and encouraged me. You all have been such a great team to work with and without your support this book would not have been possible. With gratitude and love. God bless each one of you!

To my wife Carol

To my children Matthew, Jody, Nicholas, Grace, Anne and Adam

To my grandchildren Westin, Hudson, Graceyn, Jordan, Luke, Mackenna and Drew

To my mother Mary Lou and my father and business partner Raymond Miller, Jr.

To my friend Jeanne Hofmann

To my nephew Danny Ciurczak

To my business associate Paul Prizer

INTRODUCTION

If you have read *Taming Chaos – A Parable on Decision-Making* and are now beginning to read this *Leader's Discussion Guide & Workbook*: Congratulations! You've already taken a crucial first step towards helping teenagers and young adults nurture, grow and understand the process of decision-making, which is a "critical thinking" skill for making real-life decisions. *Taming CHAOS* was written to teach young people to engage bravely when facing difficult choices, from both a subjective and objective perspective. This parable provides specific steps and a process for evaluating and quantifying uncertainty and moving forward with confidence and courage. Understanding the "Decision-Making" process will encourage and enable teenagers and young adults to learn when taking a risk is worth it. After reading *Taming CHAOS*, teenagers will realize and conclude they are better prepared and equipped to tackle many of life's difficult challenges. This will lead to developing and growing healthier families, leading to a stronger, more enlightened and inspired society.

We often hear and read about how American students are lagging behind in essential "critical thinking" skills, from reading, writing and speaking to quantitative, scientific and technical reasoning. Decision-making is a fundamental life skill which must be formally taught. The ability to choose wisely and make excellent decisions cannot be viewed in a static fashion, separate from the core components of any academic curriculum. Instead, decision-making must be understood to be dynamic and inextricably woven into the fabric of the foundational areas of academic study: from English, Literature, Language Arts and Social Sciences to Science, Mathematics and Technology.

Making sound decisions is a process of both analyzing objective facts and data and evaluating and weighing subjective experiences. Students who develop strong competency in decision-making will be able to apply this discipline in all areas of their lives, in school, at home and their daily activities and routines. A teenager or young adult who has strengthened their decision-making skills will be able to read *Romeo and Juliet* with greater appreciation for the societal and emotional pressures influencing the young couple. Teenagers will be able to look at data gathered from fruit fly phenotypes with greater appreciation for the scientific method and a more discerning eye for how to test the experiment's hypothesis. Young adults will be able to examine a geometric proof and think more logically about how each subsequent step builds on the previous one.

Whether you teach or lead discussions in Reading, Writing, Language Arts, Social Studies, Life Skills, Science, Math or Technology, *Taming CHAOS* can be integrated seamlessly into your current academic curriculum and educational programs. *Taming CHAOS* is intended to teach the discipline of "Decision-Making" to teenagers and young adults.

The teenage middle school years are absolutely vital to shaping life skills for a fruitful, stable, and contributing adulthood. Science is continually revealing that the brains of young people between the ages of ten and twenty-four are still growing—and, as a result, are particularly vulnerable to the consequences of poor decision-making. The adolescent brain is practically hard-wired to take dangerous and uncalculated risks, socially and physically, not always in their best interest.

As young people develop their identities and discover the world and their place within it, they are naturally inclined to experiment. Young brains have immature systems for both processing consequences and rewards and keeping impulses in check long enough to make reasoned, logical and sound decisions.

This means that on a neurological level, teenagers are far more inclined to act impulsively than adults. This has been confirmed by researchers at University College London's Institute of Cognitive Neuroscience, who found that as compared to men, fourteen-year-old boys chose risky options more often when playing video games, and got a bigger "emotional charge" when the risks they took yielded a win or a favorable outcome. Psychologists at Temple University found that these results were amplified when teenagers were among friends—when they played video games in groups, they became even more sensitive to potential rewards from taking risks.

The science and research is clear: Teenage brains are attuned to seek thrills and rewards, and they do this by tolerating a higher degree of risk than adult brains. At the same time; however, teenage brains also become more easily overwhelmed by "information overload" than adult brains. We live in an age when young adults are constantly stimulated, from high-stakes classroom and extracurricular environments, to family homes where activities are employing smartphones, computers and a variety of technology, within a setting of increasingly complex and often stressful family relationships. Essentially, teenagers today are operating with underdeveloped neurology that is stressed and overtaxed.

It's no wonder parents and educators are baffled by how to impart values and discuss the virtues of conscientiousness, rational thinking, and empathy into wired, stressed, and over-stimulated teens! This is where *Taming CHAOS* comes in.

Through an engaging and relatable story, *Taming CHAOS* teaches a step-by-step process for making good decisions. Young brains, which are so prone to overload, crave structure and discipline. This is exactly why *Taming CHAOS* breaks down the process of decision-making into six-steps that can be applied to any situation, from working through a challenging science problem in the classroom to evaluating more subjective real-life situations, particularly interpersonal ones.

Taming CHAOS is about helping your students to feel empowered within their own lives. They no longer need to surrender to the whims of their emotions when facing tough choices and challenges. They no longer need to feel at the mercy of an unknowable future. Just as adults do, they too can begin to learn to take responsibility for the consequences of their decisions. This means that they must learn to deal with the uncomfortable possibility of failure—but it also means that they can lay claim to the exciting prospect of success and influencing their own futures in a favorable way.

Teenagers and young adults who read *Taming CHAOS* will begin to realize that they have unique talents and while growing in their understanding of the gift of "free will," will be able to generate more positive energy, associated with their creative mind, that will lead to more successful and better outcomes for the benefit of others, and not just themselves. And for educators struggling to maintain classroom discipline and instill strong ethics in the next generation, this is good news indeed!

How to use this Leader's Discussion Guide and Workbook

This Leader's Discussion Guide and Workbook will follow the structure of *Taming CHAOS*. **Chapter 1** of the Leader's Discussion Guide, for example, should be read alongside **Chapter 1** of *Taming CHAOS*.

Each chapter of the Leader's Discussion Guide begins with a **Summary** section that summarizes the plot developments of the corresponding chapter in *Taming CHAOS*. This is to help you organize your thoughts quickly and easily before beginning discussions with students or study group participants.

Next you'll find a **Concepts** section, which highlights **specific concepts and skills** folded into the corresponding chapter of *Taming CHAOS*. The **Concepts** sections will present the new ideas, key concepts and vocabulary of each chapter in a condensed format, so that you can organize your lectures, class discussions or study group sessions and make sure that your participants have understood the lessons of the chapter.

Each chapter of the Leader's Discussion Guide will also offer you specific **Discussion Questions** to help you delve deeper into the challenges, choices and questions that Carly and Jimmy face—and to help teenagers and young adults not only employ and apply a decision-making process to many situations that arise in *Taming CHAOS,* but also to "real life" situations they will experience in their own lives and daily routines.

Should you wish to evaluate teenagers and young adult's comprehension of *Taming CHAOS*, the Leader's Discussion Guide will offer you possible **Evaluation Questions** that all participants can respond to in groups, at home, or in the classroom.

Finally, you'll find a **Glossary of Terms** at the end of the Leader's Discussion Guide that you can refer to as you progress through *Taming CHAOS*. Many terms in *Taming CHAOS* will be colloquially familiar to you—but they have more specific and nuanced definitions when used in the context of teaching the discipline of decision-making, growing a better understanding about the nature of "risk-taking" and "how to" quantify and evaluate uncertainty. So, ask students to be open to learning deeper definitions to words and concepts they might have thought they already understood.

You are also strongly encouraged to engage with *Taming CHAOS* and your teenagers and young adults interactively.

Use the parable of *Taming CHAOS* as a springboard for frank discussions with your students. Ask them to relate Carly and Jimmy's choices, decisions and consequences to those in their own lives. *Taming CHAOS* begins a constructive and healthy conversation with teenagers and young adults on the process of "decision-making," acknowledging that the decisions and choices they face are valid and worthy of careful consideration, just as adult decisions and choices are. Above all else: Enjoy the journey!

CHAPTER 1

Summary

Chapter 1 of *Taming CHAOS* introduces readers to the main characters, **Carly and Jimmy**, who are older sister and younger brother. As they are riding their bikes to the first day of school, they find a scared and wounded dog in hiding at the edge of the woods. The dog is very frightened and possibly aggressive.

Carly and Jimmy have to weigh several questions: Should they help the dog, even though it might be dangerous? Is it worth being late to the first day of school? How should they communicate with their school and their parents that they are going to be late?

As Carly and Jimmy wait for help to come from Animal Control, they encounter a boy they've never met before

1

who treats them rudely and suggests that they should put the dog "out of its misery." Carly and Jimmy then have to decide how to navigate this unexpected and unpleasant exchange.

Concepts

The function of **Chapter 1** is to draw young readers into the mystery that Carly and Jimmy unexpectedly find themselves. Who is this strange dog, what happened to it, and what can be done to make its life better? *Taming CHAOS* is a parable, which means that it teaches student readers by telling them a story. This early in the book, we want your students to relate to Carly and Jimmy and to feel curious about the dog they have found and the strange boy who shows up to antagonize Carly and Jimmy. I have deliberately chosen not to introduce any new concepts or terms in this first chapter—because we want student readers to start learning without even knowing it!

However, even before *Taming CHAOS* starts to teach lessons about decision-making, it is introducing the reality that we all face choices every single day. In your discussion with students about **Chapter 1**, you can begin to highlight the decisions that Carly and Jimmy are making. You can also begin to highlight how Carly and Jimmy represent one approach to decision-making: Talking things over and considering the possible consequences of your actions. The boy who interrupts their conversation, however, represents a different approach: Responding automatically and impulsively to emotion.

Discussion Questions

- What *choices* do Carly and Jimmy face in this chapter?
  - ○ Should they investigate the strange sound in the bushes?
  - ○ Should they help the dog?
  - ○ *How* should they help the dog?
  - ○ How can they make the dog more comfortable?
  - ○ Should they engage with the strange boy who interrupts them?
- What *consequences* do Carly and Jimmy face as a result of their choices?
  - ○ If they spend time helping the dog, they could be late to school. The dog could also prove to be dangerous.
  - ○ If they don't help the dog, it could continue to suffer or even die.
  - ○ The strange boy who interrupts them thrusts himself into their conversation. Do they really have a choice about engaging with him? What would be the consequences of ignoring him or telling him to go away?
- If *you* found a strange, mean, hurt dog in the woods, what would *you* do?
- How would you react if a kid your age you didn't know spoke rudely to you right off the bat?

Evaluation Questions

- Who are Carly and Jimmy and what is their relationship to each other?

- Based on the text, what are some character traits of Carly and Jimmy? Use quotes from *Taming CHAOS* to support your answers.
- Describe the animal that Carly and Jimmy find in the woods. Why is this animal particularly risky?
- Describe the boy who interrupts Carly and Jimmy as they wait for Animal Control. What are some of his character traits? Support your answer with evidence from the boy's behavior.

Notes

CHAPTER 2

Summary

In **Chapter 2**, a new character arrives: **Hank**, the animal control specialist. He guesses from the animal's condition that it probably had a neglectful owner who mistreated it—and that it has probably also been hit by a car. Then, he shows Carly and Jimmy the tool and technique he uses to trap dogs humanely. He catches the dog, causing it as little distress as he can. The dog is so huge that Hank needs Carly and Jimmy's help to lift its cage into his van.

Before Hank leaves with the dog, he tells Carly and Jimmy that they did the right thing by calling Animal Control. Carly and Jimmy ask what will happen to the dog, and Hank tells

6

them that he will take the dog to the county animal shelter, where euthanasia is a possibility.

After Hank leaves, Carly and Jimmy realize they are over an hour late and have missed the first period of the first day of school. They decide not to call their parents and instead to get to school as soon as they can. They also realize that they feel very worried about the dog's possible fate, and they resolve to ask their parents to take them to the animal shelter to check on the dog when they get home from school.

Concepts

Like **Chapter 1**, **Chapter 2** of *Taming CHAOS* aims to engross students in Carly and Jimmy's story and the process of making decisions before they realize that they are learning specific concepts. However, this chapter does begin to emphasize that decisions have consequences—and that those consequences are not always clearly *favorable or unfavorable*. Decision-making is so challenging because most decisions have mixed outcomes: We might like part of a given result, and dislike another part.

So, while Carly and Jimmy are relieved that the dog is temporarily safe, they realize that it is still in peril, just in a different way. They also have to cope with the fact that while they saved the dog from the certain peril of dying in the woods, they are responsible for putting the dog in uncertain circumstances of the shelter. They have to cope with the gray area that their decision creates.

They also have to confront the consequences of their decision to be late to school. Ultimately, they decide *not to communicate* with their parents about what has happened to them, in favor of getting to school as fast as they can. They have chosen to *do nothing*—which is a choice in and of itself. As we'll see later in the book, this decision too has consequences.

Discussion Questions

- By helping the dog, Carly and Jimmy inadvertently create a new danger for it. What risk does the dog face at the animal shelter?
- Why does the shelter have to resort to euthanasia for certain animals? In your mind, is it *just* to euthanize some animals so that resources can be focused on more adoptable animals?
- Now that you know the consequences of their actions, do you think Carly and Jimmy did the right thing by calling animal control?
- What would you do if you had chosen to be late to school for a reason that you thought was justifiable? Should Carly and Jimmy have called their parents before heading to school? Or was it more important for them to get to school as soon as possible?

Evaluation Questions

- Who is Hank and what is his role in the story?
- What important information does Hank give Carly and Jimmy about the dog's condition?
- Does Hank think Carly and Jimmy did the right thing by calling him? Support your answer with evidence from Hank's dialogue.

- What could happen to the dog once it gets to the county animal shelter? In your opinion, are Carly and Jimmy now "responsible" for the dog?

Notes

CHAPTER 3

Summary

Chapter 3 introduces the reader to several new and important characters. We meet Carly and Jimmy's parents, **Pete**, a middle school principal, and **Kim**, a risk management consultant and professor. We also meet the veterinarian in charge of the stray dog's care, **Dr. John Ancona**. And, we learn that the abrasive kid Carly and Jimmy met earlier is in fact their new next-door neighbor **Lonnie**, who used to attend the middle school where their father Pete is principal.

This chapter is all about introducing young readers to the concept of confronting the consequences of one's decisions. Carly and Jimmy sit down with their parents and have a frank discussion about how their decisions in the previous chapters affected the family. We learn that even though Carly and Jimmy meant no harm, their decision not to communicate with their parents about where they were and why they were late to school caused a great deal of concern. Ultimately, Pete and Kim agree with Carly and Jimmy's decision to help the dog, but they disagree with *how* Carly and Jimmy executed that decision.

The chapter ends at the animal shelter, where we learn that the dog has a broken foreleg, probably from being struck by a car. Dr. Ancona tells the family honestly that he would usually euthanize a stray dog under these circumstances. Carly and Jimmy ask their parents for a family meeting to decide if they should adopt the dog and take on the responsibility for the dog's treatment.

We learn that Kim has a specific **Decision-Making Process** that she teaches her students and clients. Using a **whiteboard**, Kim helps people assess the risks involved in their choices. The family decides to use the whiteboard to come to a decision about adopting the dog.

Concepts

This chapter begins the introduction of two very important aspects of the decision-making: **empathy** and **consequences**. We don't yet define these terms specifically, but **Chapter 3** lays the groundwork for students to begin to consider their relevance.

Empathy is introduced in the initial exchange between Carly and Jimmy and their dad Pete, who tells them that Lonnie has had some struggles in the recent past. Carly and Jimmy are both hurt, frustrated, and shocked by Lonnie's attitude and behavior towards them and towards the dog they found, and Pete begins to introduce the concept of considering the situation from Lonnie's perspective and realizing that there may be more at play than meets the eye.

We then begin to consider **consequences** as Carly and Jimmy sit down with their parents to discuss why they were late to school. Ultimately, Pete and Kim are not upset about the decision that Carly and Jimmy made about the dog—they just wish that Carly and Jimmy had communicated with them about where they were and what they were doing. In the conversation between the siblings and their parents, students will start to see that decision-making involves both thinking ahead to imagine the future ramifications of one's actions and also using one's imagination to consider how one's actions could impact others.

Carly voices the chapter's **primary theme**: "We don't have to just guess at an answer based on our fear and worry." **Chapter 3** lays the foundation for students to learn a step-by-step **Decision-Making Process** that takes the guesswork and impulsiveness out of making choices, and instead gives students a clear framework for thinking rationally about how they want to act in the world.

Discussion Questions

- Have you ever been in a situation where someone did something unkind to you or hurt your feelings and you didn't understand why? How would learning more about that person's history and possible intentions change how you felt about the situation?

- If you were in Carly and Jimmy's shoes, and you found out that an animal you cared about might be put down, how might you convince your parents to consider adopting the dog? Would you beg and plead? Would you try to get them to see your point of view? Do you have a family meeting routine?

- Why is it important for the family to take an evening to come to a decision? How might stepping back and taking time to discuss the situation benefit the family?

Evaluation Questions

- Who are Pete and Kim, and what do they do for a living?
  - We know this parable is about decision-making. How does decision-making play a role in both Pete and Kim's careers?

- Who is Lonnie? What is his relationship to Pete? What do we learn about Lonnie in **Chapter 3** that might have influenced his rude behavior toward Carly and Jimmy in **Chapter 1**?

- Now that the dog has been examined at the animal shelter, we know a little more about it. Is it male or female? What is its condition? What does Dr. John Ancona think might have happened to it just before Carly and Jimmy found it? What is his final recommendation for what should be done with the dog?

- Carly and Jimmy's family uses a specific tool to help with family discussions. What is that tool?

Notes

CHAPTER 4

Summary

In **Chapter 4**, we join the family around the **whiteboard**, where they are busily discussing what to do about the dog. This chapter takes a step back from the plot of the parable and begins to introduce concepts related to decision-making through the family's conversation. Kim—and sometimes Pete—takes the helm of explaining concepts to Carly and Jimmy, who ask questions to help flesh out ideas. Carly and Jimmy's questions are specifically tailored to mirror the questions your students might bring up.

The family tackles the decision of whether or not to adopt the dog by thinking about the actual situation, and also by considering hypothetical situations that help illustrate decision-making concepts.

Concepts

In this chapter, Kim introduces a specific process called the **Six Steps of Risk Management**. It can also be called the **Six Steps of the Decision-Making Process**. Make sure that your students understand that **risk management** and **decision-making** are interchangeable ideas because, ultimately, all decisions will involve some risk or uncertainty and coming to the right decision for you involves analyzing and managing these unknowns.

We learn **Steps 1 through 3** of the **Six Steps of Risk Management** in this chapter:

The Six Steps of Risk Management
Or The Six Steps of the Decision-Making Process

Step 1: Identification

- What is the question you are trying to answer or the problem you are trying to solve? This might seem like an obvious first step, but sometimes we aren't actually sure what specifically is causing us to struggle. We can't solve a problem until we have defined it in specific terms. Similar to planning a trip, if we do not know our starting point or origin, we will never be successful in charting a path to our destination.

- Consider the possible **consequences** or **outcomes** of each possible course of **action** you could take to respond to the problem. A consequence or outcome is an event, observation, or circumstance, whether subjective or objective, that occurs as a result of an action (or as a result of inaction).

- Outcomes often come in the form of **costs**. Costs are not always financial; they can involve money, time, effort, and/or emotional investment.

Step 2: Determine Subjective and Objective Risks

- **Subjective risks** are risks that we perceive to be present based on our feelings, intuition or gut instinct, and past experience.
  - ○ The subjective risks we perceive to be involved in a situation are influenced by how **familiar** we are with the situation and how much **control** we think we have over the situation.
- **Objective risks** are uncertainties or risks that can be physically measured or quantified in terms of numbers, statistics or facts.
  - ○ We can objectively measure the **frequency** and **severity** of possible outcomes; however, low-frequency, high-severity outcomes might influence our subjective perception of risk.
- It is critical to take a step back and think about what you actually know about a situation, based upon its objective considerations, versus what you feel about a situation or its subjective considerations. Both considerations have their place in making a decision, but they must be considered and evaluated

separately from each other in order for you to think clearly.

Step 3: Analyze and Quantify
- Gather facts about the situation using research. Think objectively about these facts to help you analyze the possible outcomes.

Discussion Questions
- Can you think of a situation where you overestimated or underestimated the risk involved based on your *familiarity* with the situation and sense of *control* over the circumstances? (An example might be facing the first day of school as a new student in town. You are *unfamiliar* with the school/teachers/students and you cannot *control* others' behavior towards you, so you might feel a lot of anxiety—that ultimately proves to be unwarranted.)
- What are some real-world low-frequency, high-severity outcomes that distort our perception of risk? (These might include natural disasters, plane crashes, etc.) What are some risks that are actually more imminent that receive less media attention because they are less sensational? (Flu, auto accidents, etc.)

Evaluation Questions
- Either in groups or individually, ask your students to come up with a fictional problem or a decision they could imagine themselves having to face in their real

lives. This should be a problem that they are comfortable either sharing with the class or with you (depending on whether you'd like to use this Evaluation Question as the basis for class discussion or simply grade their work individually). Some examples could include: Should I join the soccer team or the drama club? Should I take on summer work? What topic should I choose for a major research paper?

o If you and the students would like to tackle more challenging questions (Should I continue this difficult friendship? Should I befriend this student who has behavioral problems? Should I ask Mom for more visitation time with Dad?), go for it! But I recommend that you stress with your students they should work strictly with fictional problems and not include details from their actual lives that might be sensitive for them or for people they care about.

- Have the students go through the first three steps of the Decision-Making Process using their hypothetical problem/question. This can be done in discussion, using a blackboard or whiteboard; or, the assignment can be completed more formally, using a written report, outline, or essay.

Notes

CHAPTER 5

Summary

Chapter 5 presents the second half of the family meeting that started in **Chapter 4**. It is structured very similarly to **Chapter 4**, in that teaching moments are folded into the family's conversation, with Kim and Pete explaining concepts and Carly and Jimmy asking questions that might reflect the kinds of questions your students will have.

By the end of the chapter, using the Decision-Making Process, the family decides to adopt the dog for a one-month trial period. This will allow them to see how she fits in with the family—and how the family fits in with her. Carly and Jimmy have agreed to help with the dog's care, both through their time and effort and in terms of their money. The family has come up with a plan for what to do if the dog proves to be untrainable and cannot stay with them past the one-month trial.

Concepts

This chapter introduces the critical decision-making concept of **free will**, which is the ability to act and make choices employing one's own discretion, without being constrained or manipulated by outside influences.

This is a key concept for students to understand. So often, young people feel like they are at the mercy of influences larger than themselves and that their internal compass in the world doesn't matter. Taken to its logical extreme, this attitude can lead to behavioral problems and ultimately a lack of confidence in oneself or a failure to give consideration to others. I recommend discussing the idea of free will with your students at length—even though many adults take this concept for granted, it is often a new consideration for young people.

Help your students understand how their free will involves both freedom—they do have some degree of control over the outcomes of their lives—and also responsibility—they must bear the consequences of their own actions. Some of the questions in the Discussion Questions section below will help you get the ball rolling.

As **Chapter 5** continues, we learn **Steps 4 through 6** of the **Decision-Making Process**:

The Six Steps of Risk Management
Or The Six Steps of the Decision-Making Process

Step 4: Rank or Prioritize the Options

- You now have enough information—both subjective and objective—about the possible courses of action to decide how much risk you are willing to take in exchange for what kinds of rewards.

- It is rare that a single course of action yields to no consequence at all. It is more common to expect multiple consequences from a decision. When faced with multiple possibilities or outcomes, it is best to develop a ranking of all the possibilities, so one can sort through all of the multiple outcomes and make a decision that will be consistent with determining the smallest financial consequence and least amount of uncertainty.

- As you'll notice in the parable, as the family is discussing Step 4, they realize that they overlooked a possible course of action: a compromise between adopting the dog forever and leaving her at the shelter to be euthanized. They realize they can adopt her for a trial period, which will help them gather more information about her to make a stronger permanent decision. This is an important point to highlight in your discussion with students: The process of working through Steps 1 through 6 often clarifies a situation, so that new ideas arise that might not otherwise have been considered.

Step 5: Make a Choice and Act on It

- Based on the process you've gone through in Steps 1 through 4, it's time to pick the course of action that suits your needs as closely as possible—and then act on it.

Step 6: Evaluate and Adjust

- Students are often surprised to learn that there is still a sixth step after they have made a choice and carried it out. However, it is always critical to learn from one's actions—and it is rarely too late to make adjustments. Once a course of action has been taken, compare the real-life outcomes with the hypothetical outcomes developed from the brainstorming during the Decision-Making Process. If adjustments can be made to minimize further risk or maximize future rewards, go for it!

Discussion Questions

- What does free will mean to you, in your own words?
- How do you know you have free will? Give an example of a time in your life when you faced a choice, and you exercised your free will. Did the situation turn out favorably or unfavorably? Did you adjust accordingly?
- Why is the concept of free will in some ways similar in feeling to one finally experiencing complete freedom, no longer chained down in bondage?
- What responsibilities come with having free will?

Evaluation Questions

- Have your students revisit, either individually or in groups, the hypothetical problem or question they developed after reading **Chapter 4**. They should continue their project of working through the Six Steps of the Decision-Making Process to come to a decision for how they would act if they were actually faced with this problem.

• Ask students to use their imaginations to think through **Step 6**. Does everything work out according to plan? What is the largest curveball the universe could possibly throw at them—and how would they adjust if it did? For fun, students or groups can even trade their projects, evaluate each other's work, and present each other with possible outcomes for the decisions they've made. This will allow students to arrive at Step 6 with fresh eyes taking notice, with excitement, of the outcomes from their decisions.

Notes

CHAPTER 6

Summary

The family goes to pick up the dog in **Chapter 6**. They learn from Dr. John Ancona that she probably has some sheep dog in her, and possibly some Mastiff and Chow–Chow. Post-surgery (Dr. Ancona has reset her broken foreleg) and now totally clean, CHAOS is much less intimidating—although very large.

Dr. Ancona gives the family some pointers about caring for a dog with a difficult history. He will remain in contact with the family for the rest of the story to help advise them on caring for the dog. It's important to emphasize this with students: When dealing with strange animals, it's always necessary to have expert help.

This story has a happy ending, but there are some animals that simply are not safe for adoption, so please make sure that your students understand that Carly, Jimmy, and their parents have not made any decisions about the dog without a lot of consideration, and that Dr. Ancona and the shelter staff would not allow the dog to go home with them if they were not confident that she would make a safe pet. Based on Dr. Ancona's advice, the family agrees to give the dog lots of time and space to heal from her surgery and to get used to her new environment.

Carly comes up with the name CHAOS for the dog—an acronym for *Choices About Objective and Subjective risk*, which is a great way for students to remember all that they've learned.

As the family drives to and from the animal hospital to pick up CHAOS and bring her home, Kim introduces some more decision-making concepts.

At the end of the chapter, Lonnie shows up again, and is once again rude and dismissive—particularly when he learns that the family has decided to adopt the dog, which he clearly doesn't like.

Concepts

This chapter gives a little background history on how decision-making has changed as human knowledge and understanding have deepened throughout history. It isn't important for students to learn the names and dates of this historical trajectory—unless you want to partner up with your grade's History teacher and create a specific lesson on the topic.

The most important thing for students to come away understanding is that decision-making used to involve a lot of guesswork, and that human beings used to feel very much at the mercy of the whims of mythological deities. Once numerical systems were invented, **quantitative calculations** and most importantly **statistics** gave people a much more objective basis for making rational decisions based on past experience.

If you are teaching *Taming CHAOS* as part of a Math class, or if you are an English teacher teaming up with the Math teacher, **Chapter 6** is your opportunity to fold in skills surrounding statistics. Have students plot data on a graph and draw a **bell curve** and use that bell curve to make predictions about future outcomes.

If your students have not yet studied statistics and plotting data points is beyond their skill set, you can still introduce the statistical concepts of this chapter in general terms, as Kim and Pete do. The important concepts for students to remember are:

- The difference between **possibilities**—possible outcomes—and **probabilities**—how likely possible outcomes are to occur;

- The purpose of a **bell curve** or **normal distribution:** It is simply a way of graphically depicting data that helps you draw conclusions that can be used in forecasting future outcomes or scenarios;

- The **law of large numbers:** If you have encountered a scenario a large number of times in the past, you might be able to draw reasonable conclusions about what *could* happen in the future based on what has happened in the past. Emphasize that predicting the future with absolute certainty is impossible, and **outlier** events that do not follow data predictions should be expected or can and will occur.

- This chapter also stresses that, at the middle school level, the terms **risk** and **uncertainty** can be used interchangeably. Students that advance in the field of risk management will eventually learn and become familiar with these terms, but for the time being, the *nature of risk* and *uncertainty* are similar.

Discussion Questions

- How often do you use numbers, symbols and figures in making decisions? When you don't use **quantitative calculations** to help guide you, what else do you rely on? Your intuition? Past experience?

- Have you found that your intuition is a reliable guide for decision-making? If you had a more reliable tool— even if it required a little more mental focus and self–discipline and more time—would you use it?

Evaluation Questions

- What does the name CHAOS stand for?
- How did human beings make decisions before they had a counting or numbering system?
- Where did the earliest numbering systems come from?
- How did numbering systems change the way that human beings make decisions?

- Explain the difference between *possibilities* and *probabilities* in your own words.
- Can the *law of large numbers* be used to predict the future? How? What are its limitations?

Notes

CHAPTER 7

Summary

Because **Chapters 4**, **5**, and **6** place a lot of emphasis on teaching detailed decision-making concepts, **Chapter 7** aims to draw students back into the narrative of CHAOS the dog and her blossoming friendship with Carly and Jimmy. We discover in this chapter that it is a challenge to earn the trust of a dog that has had unfavorable experiences with humans in the past, and we witness Carly and Jimmy making small steps to make CHAOS feel at ease in their company.

Just as CHAOS needs to be "handled with care," we learn in this chapter that the same thing applies to Lonnie. Like CHAOS, he has had very difficult past experiences that now explain his current behavior and his level of trust with new people. Carly and Jimmy are both surprised to learn from Lonnie that his father adopted a dog named Rex, who, like CHAOS, is anxious around people. Because Lonnie's relationship with his dad is so fragile and complex, the history of Rex might explain why Lonnie was so hostile towards CHAOS.

Concepts

The main decision-making concept that Kim introduces in **Chapter 7** is that of **perils** and **hazards**. A peril is a circumstance that could causes a loss, and a hazard is anything that increases the probability or likelihood of that loss occurring. Kim illustrates the difference with the idea of walking a tightrope, which is, in and of itself, full of risk and uncertainty: The tightrope walker could fall and become injured, which would be a loss. If the rope is not properly tightened, this would be a hazard, because it would increase the chance of the tightrope walker falling.

Discussion Questions

- Do you have any personal experience working with a shy or nervous animal? How about just training any animal, in general? (This is an opportunity for students to share personal experiences that might help them relate to Carly and Jimmy's experience with CHAOS.)
- **Chapter 7** introduces the concepts of *peril* and *hazard*. Have you ever faced a peril in your life? What hazards were involved—or could have been involved?
- In **Chapter 7**, we get some clues about Lonnie's past that help explain why he dislikes CHAOS so much. How does Carly and Jimmy's attitude toward Lonnie

change as he reveals his experience with his dad's dog Rex? Have you ever changed your mind about someone, or at least felt that you understood them better, once you learned more about them and their past experiences?

Evaluation Questions

- Have students work individually or in groups to come up with a list of hypothetical situations employing possible perils (these could be anything from crossing the street to taking a test).

- Ask students to trade their list of perils with other students. The new students will then add *hazards* to the situations originally described by their classmates. (For example, if the first student describes the peril of taking a test, the next student might add to the situation the hazard of not having gotten enough sleep the night before.)

- Who is Rex? What is his relationship to Lonnie?

- How does Lonnie's past experience with Rex influence how he reacts to CHAOS? Think about Lonnie's behavior in **Chapter 7**, and also think about his behavior in previous chapters.

Notes

CHAPTER 8

Summary

In **Chapter 8**, Carly and Jimmy tell their parents about their conversation with Lonnie. Carly highlights a striking thing Lonnie said: "My dad loves his dumb old dog more than me." Carly and Jimmy and their parents agree that Lonnie's complicated feelings about his dad are probably influencing his behavior toward Carly and Jimmy.

This leads to both Carly and Jimmy wanting to make an effort to get to know Lonnie better and give him a chance. The family decides to use the whiteboard to make a decision about whether the siblings should risk extending an offer of friendship to Lonnie.

This chapter illustrates how the Decision-Making Process can be applied to situations that are not always "clear cut"- and quantitative in nature, but involve a lot of subjectivity. By the end of the family discussion, Carly and Jimmy have resolved to include Lonnie more, in an effort to become his friend. Kim and Pete caution Carly and Jimmy to be aware that Lonnie is "a person, not a project," and that he has free will with his considerations too. He could very well reject Carly and Jimmy, and he would be within his rights to do so.

Concepts

This chapter expands significantly on the concept of **free will**. Kim tells the kids that using our free will introduces a large responsibility into the equation: "We have to consider more than just our own desires; we also have to consider *who we're called to be* as human beings. We have to think about how our choices might affect other people and shape the future."

Chapter 8 represents a major turning point in *Taming CHAOS*. Until this chapter, we have been teaching students basic skills of decision-making. In Chapter 8, we begin to pull back and take a bird's eye view. *Why* is decision-making so important? It's not enough just to learn the *how-to*; it's critical that students put these skills in context, and understand that strong decision-making will profoundly impact every aspect of their lives, because it is so inextricably linked to how they relate to other people and how they function as contributing members of society.

This chapter opens the door for you to have a conversation with students about where their values come from and how they can strengthen and sustain these values. Kim puts it in terms of everyone having a decision-making **compass**, based upon their upbringing and the values instilled in them by their families, and strengthened by both the objective and subjective experiences of their lives.

This chapter also introduces a few new terms. The first among these is **status quo**—the way things have always been. As students read this chapter and think about the choice Carly and Jimmy have with regard to befriending Lonnie, they should start to realize that each decision they make in life in some way affects whether they will maintain their personal status quo or whether they will grow as individuals.

Often, students will see from this chapter, we are confronted with **temptations**, which seem appealing in the moment, but do not actually help us grow over the long term. And, even when using the Decision-Making Process, the "right or wrong" answer will not always be black and white, requiring us to take a **leap of faith**.

Pete sums up these ideas with a quote from the West Point Cadet Prayer that guide cadets at West Point: "*Make us to choose the harder right, instead of the easier wrong.*"

Chapter 8 ultimately makes the point that decision-making is not just about using hard skills to make choices in the moment. It is about approaching life with purpose and integrity, so that we can continually grow to become the person that we are meant to be.

Discussion Questions

- Take some time to think about *who you are* and *what do you value?* What in your life is worth standing up for or paying the price? What gives you meaning? Ask each student to answer the question "Who am I?"

- How do your values influence how you make decisions? Do you always consider your values when you face a tough decision, or do you sometimes allow yourself to be swayed by temptation? (This is a trick question: We *all* get swayed by temptation.)

- How can we work to strengthen our decision-making "compass"?

Evaluation Questions

- What does the term **status quo** mean? On its own, is the status quo a favorable or an unfavorable concept? Or is it neutral?

- Explain the concept of **temptation** in your own words. Is it possible to make a decision that has favorable short-term outcomes and unfavorable long-term outcomes? Give an example of this kind of decision.

- Explain what the quote, *"Make us to choose the harder right, instead of the easier wrong"* means in your own words. Can you think of a situation in your own life that this quote might apply?

- Carly points out that most of the risks associated with befriending Lonnie are *subjective*. Can Carly and Jimmy still use the Six Steps of Risk Management to make a decision? How does using this process change when there are less objective facts and quantitative calculations, and more emotions and interpersonal considerations to be factored in?

Notes

CHAPTER 9

Summary

Chapter 9 begins with Carly and Jimmy trying to get CHAOS, who has begun to adjust to the family but is still nervous about the neighborhood, to take a walk around the block. Lonnie shows up, and Carly and Jimmy are able to test their decision to be kind to him and see if they can initiate a friendship.

As it turns out, Lonnie knows a little about dog training from his experience with Rex, his dad's dog. He gives Carly and Jimmy some pointers—emphasizing that they need to be extremely patient, because progress with a dog like CHAOS will be incremental. After a small success getting CHAOS to venture a few feet away from the family's front yard, Lonnie seems to have warmed up to Carly and Jimmy a bit. He confesses to them that his father is an alcoholic.

Carly and Jimmy thank Lonnie for his help with CHAOS, and Lonnie apologizes to Carly and Jimmy for his prior behavior.

Concepts

This chapter is primarily about returning students to the characters and the story, so that they begin to see how the practical lessons they have been learning play out in interpersonal situations. There are no new decision-making concepts presented in **Chapter 9**; however, the chapter does reemphasize some ideas that will reinforce the importance of what students have learned in prior chapters.

Highlight for your students the fact that Lonnie teaches Carly and Jimmy that CHAOS's progress will be very slow and incremental. This is both factually true of training anxious dogs and is also a useful metaphor for your students' progress as they integrate the Decision-Making Process into their daily lives. Progress doesn't have to be immediate. It's better to build a habit over time than to try to make a drastic change in one day and risk becoming overwhelmed and abandoning the endeavor altogether.

The chapter closes by reinforcing the concept of the **leap of faith**, which was first introduced in **Chapter 8**. It is crucial that students do not come away from reading *Taming CHAOS* believing that life will always be predictable or that they will always have control over the outcomes of the decisions and choices they routinely make in life. We cannot predict the future, and life will throw us curveballs. Decision-making is about approaching difficult choices more rationally, rather than relying strictly on instincts, which can often times lead us down the wrong path. However, we must always consider the prospects that not all outcomes can be predicted. Despite careful planning, we must grow to recognize that the "unexpected" will occur and that on occasion we will not be in a position to accurately predict the expected outcomes of our decisions or choices.

Lonnie also brings up his father's alcoholism in this chapter and its unfavorable consequences for his family. If your school has a substance-abuse curriculum, or a program like the D.A.R.E. program, you might want to draw a link between skills students have learned through these programs and skills presented in *Taming CHAOS*. The Decision-Making Process is a *real world tool*, not a theoretical concept. It can help students navigate some of the most dangerous perils in the lives of adolescents, including drugs, alcohol, sexual behavior, the dark side of social media, bullying and the risks associated with the inexperienced teen driver.

Discussion Questions

- The approach to training and "taming" CHAOS that Lonnie teaches Carly and Jimmy is in some ways analogous to the learning process any human being undergoes when mastering a new skill. Think about what you have been learning as you read *Taming CHAOS*. How have you grown and progressed in adopting the Decision-Making Process that mirrors

CHAOS's steps toward becoming more comfortable with her new life?

Evaluation Questions

- Lonnie teaches Carly and Jimmy how to tame CHAOS using *positive reinforcement*. Describe what positive reinforcement entails.

- As Lonnie gets more comfortable with Carly and Jimmy, he reveals new information about his family life. What is this new information? How might this help explain Lonnie's past behavior toward Carly and Jimmy?

Notes

CHAPTER 10

Summary

In **Chapter 10**, the family realizes that their one-month trial period of caring for CHAOS is over, so they return to Step 6 of the Decision-Making Process: They **evaluate** what has happened. Together, they decide to keep CHAOS permanently.

This involves adjusting their agreement—there will be additional costs to caring for CHAOS permanently that weren't discussed when the family was only caring for her temporarily. The family returns to Step 1 of the Decision-Making Process to work out how to approach CHAOS's ongoing care. As they proceed through the steps, they realize that they can purchase pet insurance to help cover the costs of CHAOS's care. This discovery opens the door for Kim and Pete to teach Carly and

Jimmy some new decision-making concepts with employing the use of insurance.

Concepts

At this point in the story of *Taming CHAOS*, it will be useful to you in your discussion with students to pause and reiterate for them that *making decisions and managing risk are essentially the same thing.*

Before **Chapter 10**, *Taming CHAOS* has focused on general concepts of decision-making that are applicable to the everyday lives of middle school aged children. **Chapter 10** offers you the opportunity to start focusing upon the field of study or academic discipline known as risk management. and introducing concepts that will help prepare students for adulthood and becoming a contributing member of society at home, in the community and the workplace.

It's time to present to students the idea that risk and uncertainty can be broken down into four risk types or categories:

- **People:** the risk of injury, illness, even death.
- **Property:** the risk of damage, loss or "loss of use" of property.
- **Legal Liability:** the risk of being held legally responsible for the negligent action or inaction that results in injury or harm caused to another person or their property that would normally be expected in "civil law" using the "reasonable prudent person" rule of human behavior and enforced in a court of law. The risk types of "People

and Property" are usually fairly familiar and easy for students to conceptualize. The Legal Liability risk type will demand a more detailed and longer discussion for students to learn and understand. Everyone must live and abide by the "rule of law." If we fail to do so (whether *knowingly or unknowingly*) and our failure to follow the rules causes injury or harm to people or property, we might be legally liable for the financial cost of such injury or harm. An example of this is if a doctor prescribes the wrong medication to a patient, and the patient becomes ill, the doctor might be held liable and have to pay for that patient's treatment, lost time at work, or even *"pain and suffering,"* otherwise known as *"non–economic damages."*

- **Consequential Loss:** Financial loss that develops in one of the 3 risk types indicated above (People, Property, or Legal Lability) as a result of not managing risk effectively often times results in additional "indirect or consequential loss," representing significant financial costs and consequences greater than the "direct loss" often associated with the risk types of People, Property, or Legal Lability. An individual, a family, or a business might incur "direct costs" (paying for injury or harm caused to others, paying to repair or replace their property, or paying legal fees and legal liability damages). From there, they might also experience additional "indirect costs," which are more difficult to quantify and which tend to be exponential or multiples in relation to the "direct costs of financial harm or loss expenses." Insurance policies often describe these as "Loss of Income or Extra Expenses" as a result of an interruption of business or a consequential "loss of use" of property, injury to people or legal liability imposed by our civil laws.

o Here's an example. Say a head of household contracts a terminal illness. The "direct costs of loss" related to the death of a loved one would include the cost of medication, treatment, hospitalization, and eventual funeral expenses for that head of household. "Indirect costs or Consequential Loss" would include the loss of the head of household's income and the increased living expenses to the family due to the absence of the "head of household." Additionally, the emotional scar and feelings of brokenness–the loss of love and affection, sense of humor, emotional support, guidance for children, etc. always expected and experienced and certainly very difficult to quantify objectively. It is quite common to fail and recognize these "indirect financial costs" or often underestimate these financial costs and other related consequential financial loss.

So, the student must learn that in order to effectively manage risk and uncertainty and prepare and make provisions for the potential adverse financial consequences before they happen, 3 alternative methods to manage risk must be considered:

- **Risk Avoidance:** Is the possible consequence so great that the best course of action is just to steer clear of it altogether? Is it *possible* to avoid the risk entirely? Please teach the student that not all risk can be avoided, as in life we always will have some "inherent or residual risk" that can never be avoided or eliminated, as there is no such condition as a "risk free" existence.

- **Risk Control:** Much of the parable of *Taming CHAOS* is associated with the use of "Risk Control" in managing the uncertainties with taming CHAOS. Since the family has decided to assume the risks and financial costs of caring for CHAOS, can they minimize or reduce the unfavorable consequences of that choice? As "Risk Control" employs methods of "loss reduction" or "loss prevention," what can the family decide and plan to do to reduce the costs of the care in keeping CHAOS or prevent any future, unnecessary financial costs as CHAOS is nurtured back to good health and a normal routine. The decision to take and care for CHAOS for only a one-month trial defines the time period for 30 days, which obviously limits the "direct costs" for a certain period of time. Making certain that CHAOS gets sufficient rest, adequate exercise, nutritional meals, love and affection are good examples of risk control. Periodic bathing and washing of CHAOS, checking for ticks or fleas, proper grooming are also examples of loss prevention risk control techniques.

  o Another example of risk control that might help your students get their heads around the concept is to imagine the risk of fire. We know that installing a sprinkler system in a building to immediately provide a stream of water on a fire as soon as it is detected is not going to completely eliminate fire damage to the building, but it will certainly reduce the loss of the building's structural integrity of the building, which in the long run preserves the building, thereby reducing the costs associated with a total building loss as compared to the costs of renovation to a partially damaged building. So this significantly *controls* the risk of property damage, although it doesn't *eliminate* it.

- **Risk Financing:** *Either* (1) an individual, family, or business makes provisions to set aside financial resources that would be sufficient to cover the financial costs of a severe, catastrophic, and unexpected events; *or* (2) an individual, family, or business decides to transfer the financial responsibility for the financials cost of a severe, catastrophic, and unexpected events to an external business such as an insurance company, with the consideration of a much smaller financial outlay of money, often known as an insurance premium, because an insurance company is financially more capable of managing these significant financial consequences, with their ability to spread these "costs of risk" through the use of a "risk pooling" of many people who also decide to buy insurance and pay a smaller insurance premium.

o   Here's an example: A hurricane can wipe out a home in one day. When a family buys a house, they have no way of predicting if or when a hurricane might strike. Maybe a hurricane will never come along! But if one does . . . should the family risk losing their home? The family can choose between always keeping an extra $500,000 in the bank so they are ready to rebuild at any moment, or paying a much smaller amount to an insurance company once a month (this amount is called a **premium**) in exchange for the insurance company's agreement to cover the cost of repairing or rebuilding should a hurricane occur.

Getting specific about insurance: Students should learn to think of insurance as a risk management alternative in and of itself. When you know that you cannot afford to pay the financial cost of an unexpected significant financial loss event, that may or may not happen, you can lower your "worry value," secure "peace of mind" and help safeguard against the unfavorable financial consequences of that event by transferring the financial responsibility for the potential total loss to an insurance company.

In essence, you decide to pay a monthly **premium** in exchange for lower **worry value**—or "peace of mind." If an unfavorable event occurs that causes a loss (in the form of people, property, legal liability and/or consequential loss), you know that the insurance company will help finance this loss. If the unfavorable event never happens and there is no loss, then the student needs to understand their insurance premium has simply secured reduced "worry value" and greater "peace of mind."

Actuarial Science is a field of academic study that is the foundation for quantifying fairly, adequately and accurately the financial costs of loss and their associated perils based on the idea of spreading the costs of financial loss using a "homogeneous" pooling of many people who are like minded and desire to transfer the financial responsibility for the potential total loss to an insurance company. Insurance companies have to be prepared at any time to finance the significant financial losses incurred due to unexpected events and resulting from their unfavorable perils. Insurance companies employ **actuaries** who are trained to employ their knowledge of statistics, using the "law of large numbers," probabilities and the calculation of the "weighted average" or "expected value," which enables actuaries to quantify expected likelihoods arrayed in various ranges of frequency and severity of potential loss outcomes, so that insurance companies can offer a variety of insurance products and services, selling their products at affordable and actuarially determined fair premiums to the insurance buying public that decide to use "risk financing" as their choice to manage risk.

Chapter 10 also introduces two different kinds of risk:

- **Pure risk:** Two possible outcomes—*loss* or *no loss*.
- **Speculative Risk:** Three possible outcomes—*loss*, *no loss*, or *gain*.

Insurance is particularly important when you are facing pure risk. Have your students think back to the previous example of a hurricane. Either a hurricane occurs and damages your home (*loss*) or it does not occur and there is no resultant damage to the home (*no loss*). When you are facing pure risk, insurance is the best way to lower or reduce your "worry value"—to mitigate against the risk of whether or not a hurricane will occur. Buying insurance is not intended to be viewed as "gambling" as with "games of chance." Insurance buyers should not expect to "profit" at the time of a loss, but expect to be "restored" to their "pre–loss" condition.

The final new concept introduced in **Chapter 10** is that of **random variables**. These are chance events that may or may not occur. Purchasing insurance is a very sound financial decision for managing risk regarding the occurrence of future unexpected random loss outcomes. The family has no way of knowing, for example, whether CHAOS could get heartworm or get into another accident with a car. These would be examples of random variable loss events. Insurance is a way of financing risk surrounding random, potential and unexpected loss outcomes.

Discussion Questions

- How does the family avoid costs of risks, control the costs of risk or finance the costs of risk associated with their decision to adopt CHAOS? Are they able to eliminate risk altogether, or do they merely offset risk?

- Share with the class a situation in which you had to choose between risk avoidance and risk control. Which path did you choose? What were the results?
- Teach students to learn and recognize that in real life it is quite common to employ all 3 risk management techniques in any combination, depending on the risks or uncertainties that have been identified at the beginning of the 6 Steps of the Decision-Making Process.
- Think of some different types of insurance that you have heard of (health insurance, flood insurance, malpractice insurance). Do these types of insurance finance the costs of loss associated with the risk types of people, property, legal liability—or even consequential loss?

Evaluation Questions

- In the beginning of **Chapter 10**, we learn about how Carly, Jimmy, and Lonnie are developing a friendship. Was Carly and Jimmy's decision to befriend Lonnie a *pure risk* or a *speculative risk*? Why?
- The family finally reaches Step 6 of the Decision-Making Process—they *evaluate* their decision to adopt CHAOS for a one-month trial period. What is the result of their evaluation? What new decision do they make?
- Adopting CHAOS permanently involves new costs. What are some of these costs—in terms of time, effort, and financial resources?

- The family discovers the possibility of purchasing pet insurance for CHAOS. Is purchasing pet insurance an example of risk avoidance, risk control, or risk financing?

Notes

CHAPTER 11

Summary

At the beginning of **Chapter 11**, Jimmy brings up the difficult question of whether or not the person who hit CHAOS with their car knew that they had hit a dog—and if they did, why didn't they stop? This leads to a family discussion on the root causes of fear and ignorance, the difference between sympathy and empathy, and the role empathy plays in decision-making.

As the family is talking, Lonnie and his mother, **Abigail**, drop by. They join the conversation, and Abigail suggests that the neighborhood's security camera footage could be reviewed to find the license plate number of the car that struck CHAOS. Lonnie, Carly, and Jimmy decide to contact the security company—even though they know that bringing the person who hurt CHAOS to justice is a long shot.

The next day, the three of them speak on the phone with **Marge** and **Andrea**, representatives of the security company. Andrea, who is a manager at the company, tells them that footage is only kept for a month—which means that any footage of the accident that hurt CHAOS would already have been destroyed. The kids are temporarily disappointed and defeated.

Concepts

In this chapter, we explore the human and subjective considerations of decision-making. Kim brings up the important point that people rarely make decisions that hurt others out of sheer malice—more often they are acting out of **fear** and **ignorance**. When people are ignorant of the Decision-Making Process—when they don't know how to think through the consequences of their decisions—they can very easily fail to realize the risks they are taking, with regard to themselves or others.

This is why **empathy** is a critical skill for students to develop. This chapter teaches the important distinction between **sympathy**—the feeling for others—and **empathy**—the consideration of others needs and their feelings. Empathy is about seeking to truly understand the experiences of other people. As you discuss **Chapter 11** with your students, reinforce for them that an essential element of rationally considering risk is putting yourself in other people's shoes and thinking through how your decisions might affect them.

The concept of empathy is what underlies Lonnie, Carly, and Jimmy's motivation to try to find the driver of the car that hit CHAOS and to bring them to justice. They aren't looking for vengeance; they are seeking to dispel ignorance. As Lonnie points out, if the driver is confronted with the consequences of their action, they might be less inclined to break rules in the future.

Discussion Questions

- Explain in your own words the difference between **sympathy** and **empathy**. Give an example of a situation in which a person might be acting out of sympathy—how might their actions change if they shifted into empathy?

- Why is empathy a crucial skill for decision-making? How might the quality of our decisions be adversely affected if we fail to empathize?

- Do you agree with Lonnie, Carly, and Jimmy's reasoning when they say that the driver of the car that hit CHAOS should be brought to justice?

- Consider the role of the justice within the legal system in our country. Should justice just be about punishing guilty people, or should it serve a more complex, but useful purpose? (For example: Is it a tool for teaching the community at large and rehabilitating people who have broken the law, as Lonnie suggests?)

Evaluation Questions

- Carly asks why the driver who hit CHAOS didn't stop to help her. What is the best answer to this question that the family can come up with? Give examples from the text.

- We meet several new characters in this chapter. Who is **Abigail** and what is her relationship to Lonnie?
- Who is **Andrea Schultz**? What job does she do at the security company?
- Why can't the security company give Lonnie, Carly, and Jimmy footage of the accident that injured CHAOS?

Notes

CHAPTER 12

Summary

The kids deal with their disappointment about not being able to get the security camera footage by shifting their perspective off of the driver who hit CHAOS and back to the dog CHAOS. They redefine success under the circumstances: Maybe it's not about bringing the driver to justice, maybe it's about getting better outcomes for dogs like CHAOS. But how do they do this?

Lonnie, Carly, and Jimmy use the whiteboard and the Six Steps of the Decision-Making Process to devise an idea for helping stray and neglected dogs like CHAOS. First they have to get specific about the problem, and from there, they come up with a solution: They decide to help the animal shelter fundraise so that it can shift to a no-kill policy.

It turns out that Lonnie's mom is an executive assistant at a non-profit, which means that she has experience with this kind of fundraising. Jimmy runs next door to ask her if she'll help them brainstorm; she readily agrees. She also takes the opportunity to thank Jimmy for his friendship with Lonnie— Lonnie's behavior has turned around dramatically ever since he started to have a sense of belonging with Carly and Jimmy.

Concepts

This chapter provides a final opportunity for students to review and reinforce the Six Steps of the Decision-Making Process. It also gives a concrete example of how the Decision-Making Process can be applied to very open-ended questions, as a sort of brainstorming and idea-generating tool.

Discussion Questions

- What is the reasoning that Carly gives for shifting focus from the driver of the car back to CHAOS— and other dogs like her? Ultimately, Carly makes the point that in this situation, there is nothing that can be done about the past, so it is best to think about avoiding similar problems in the future. Do you agree with her reasoning? Have you ever been in a situation where you had to focus on looking forward rather than looking back?

- In this chapter, Lonnie, Carly, and Jimmy use the Decision-Making Process to tackle a very open-ended question. In fact, when they first get to the whiteboard, they aren't precisely sure what the problem they are addressing is. The Six Steps are not just for tackling clear-cut problems; they can also be used as a tool for helping to define problems and brainstorm solutions. How might you use this application of the Six Steps in the future?

Evaluation Questions

- Lonnie, Carly, and Jimmy work hard to do Step 1 of the Decision-Making Process—to *identify* the problem. What is the problem that they finally zero in on?
- What job does Lonnie's mother Abigail do? Why is this relevant to Lonnie, Carly, and Jimmy's project?
- What does Abigail tell Jimmy as the two of them are returning to Carly and Jimmy's house? What does this have to do with the Six Steps of the Decision-Making Process?

Notes

EPILOGUE

Summary

In the final scene of *Taming CHAOS*, we see a portrait of the end results of Lonnie, Carly, and Jimmy's most recent whiteboard decision. With Abigail's expert input, they have worked out a plan for helping the county animal shelter fundraise, through a combination of donations and earned income.

A major component of their fundraising is a small business that the three of them have started selling baseballs and tennis balls at the dog park. They contribute the proceeds of their sales to the animal shelter, so that over the course of three years, the shelter can progressively convert to a no-kill policy.

We see that Lonnie, Carly, and Jimmy feel actively engaged in their community and challenged, but inspired, by their new business, and we see the fundamental role that the Decision-Making Process played in getting them to this point.

Concepts

This **Epilogue** should help students think about how decision-making can be incorporated into their lives in a global sense. You can use the ideas in the **Epilogue** to start a conversation with students about entrepreneurism and its role in healthy communities. Highlight for your students that there is no magic ingredient for solving the animal shelter's problem. The solution requires several components, and they will take years to implement incrementally. This is another opportunity to stress the idea that the path between making a decision and turning it into a reality requires hard work and step-by-step process. Focus, discipline and attention to detail are all important considerations.

You can also use this final scene of *Taming CHAOS* to help reinforce the key concept of the book. Decision-making is not just a tool for approaching choices in the moment; it's also about having foresight about our lives and beginning to map out next steps that will help us build the careers, the families, and the lives we've always dreamed of.

Discussion Question

- How will reading *Taming CHAOS* change the way you make decisions in the future?

GLOSSARY OF TERMS

How to use this Glossary of Terms.

Many of the words in *Taming CHAOS* will already be familiar to students in a colloquial context—we all know and use words like *risk*, *possibility*, and *severity* in our day-to-day lives. However, in the context of risk management and decision-making, these terms have very specific meanings that might be different from the way we use these words more casually. As students read *Taming CHAOS* and come across unfamiliar terms—or familiar terms being used in an unfamiliar way—they can use this glossary to keep track of what these new words and phrases mean.

You'll also discover that many of the terms below have synonyms: For example, we use the words *risk* and *uncertainty* interchangeably in *Taming CHAOS*. This Glossary always mentions when a term has a synonym.

Some of the definitions below contain other terms found in this Glossary. When this occurs, these terms are set in italics, so that you can easily and quickly cross-reference definitions.

Please note that the definitions below have been adapted for students at a middle school level. Many of these terms might have a more complex definition in the context of advanced study of the academic discipline known as Risk Management.

action -the process of taking steps to make a *decision* a reality; Step 5 in the *Decision-Making Process*.

actuarial science -a field of study that involves compiling statistics and data to determine the *expected frequency* and *expected severity* of possible unfavorable events. These statistics become the basis for calculating the "pure cost of financial harm." Insurance companies use these calculations to determine insurance *premiums* for various types of *insurance*. People who practice *actuarial science* are called *actuaries*.

analysis -the process of breaking a complicated problem down into less complicated parts and looking at those parts carefully and often objectively in order to come to a *decision*; Step 3 in the *Decision-Making Process*.

bell curve -a graphical picture of actual observations that have occurred during a set period of time in which one is recording and measuring their frequency or severity. Statisticians usually refer to bell curves with the synonym *normal distribution*.

CHAOS - unknown, unexpected, disorder, abstract and confusion. In *Taming CHAOS*, Carly comes up with an *acronym* using the word "CHAOS" (an *acronym* is an abbreviation formed with the first letters of other words): **Ch**oices **A**bout **O**bjective and **S**ubjective risk.

claim - in the *insurance* industry, a request for financial compensation after someone experiences financial harm or a *loss*.

consequence -some form of harm or injury that occurs due to an event, circumstance, or peril resulting from an *action or inaction*. In *Taming CHAOS*, a synonym for *outcome*.

consultant -a person who provides expert professional advice, often to businesses or organizations about how to operate most effectively. *An advisor or counselor.*

control -the power to influence or direct how events unfold.

cost - the effort, time, or money it takes to make a *decision* a reality.

decision -the resolve to act or not act after carefully considering the factors involved in a problem. In *Taming CHAOS*, making *decisions* and managing *risk* are equivalent concepts.

Decision-Making Process -a six-step process that helps people arrive at *decisions*. This process can also be called the *Six Steps of Risk Management* because *decision-making* and *risk management* are used interchangeably in *Taming CHAOS*.

empathy - the ability to understand the needs and share the feelings of another.

evaluation -looking back at the *consequences* of an *action or inaction,* whether active or passive, to determine whether the desired result was achieved; Step 6 in the *Decision-Making Process*.

familiarity -close acquaintance with or knowledge of something, often from personal experience. *Familiarity* with an event often distorts our perception of the *risks* objectively associated with the event.

free will - the ability to act and make choices at one's own discretion without being constrained or manipulated by outside influences.

frequency - how often something occurs over a period of time.

gain -a desired benefit (like money, time, or even a subjective benefit like favorable emotions) that we receive as a *consequence* of taking a *risk*. In *Taming CHAOS*, a synonym for *reward*.

hazard -a physical condition (physical hazard), a careless attitude (morale hazard), or intent to be dishonest (moral hazard) that might increase the probability that an unfavorable outcome or financial harm or injury will occur or that might increase the frequency and/or severity of such an outcome.

identification -putting into words the problem at hand or the question one is trying to answer; Step 1 in the *Decision-Making Process*.

ignorance -lack of knowledge or information. *Ignorance* is often at the root of poor *decision-making*.

inaction -not doing anything to affect the current state of affairs. *Inaction* is just as much a choice as *action* is.

insurance -a "risk financing" *decision* or choice made by individuals—or businesses—who cannot afford to pay for the potential, expected financial harm or injury that might result from an unfavorable consequence or peril, to transfer the potential financial responsibility for harm or injury to an insurance company in exchange for "peace of mind" or lower *worry value*. These individuals or businesses choose to pay *premiums* to an insurance company to protect against *uncertainty* or *risks* to people, property, legal liabilities or consequential loss.

investment - time, money, or effort put into a situation in the hopes of receiving a *gain* in return.

law of large numbers -a statistical principle that states that we can make reasonable predictions about the future based on what has occurred frequently, or a large number of times in the past.

leap of faith -making a *decision* without reason or logical assurance of the *outcome*.

loss -an unfavorable outcome, harm or injury in which time, money, or effort is irretrievably spent as a result of taking a *risk*.

normal distribution -a visual map used in the field of statistics that shows which events happen most frequently and which happen less frequently. In *Taming CHAOS*, a synonym for *bell curve*.

objective risk -*uncertainty* or *risk* that can be physically measured or quantified in terms of numbers, statistics or facts.

offset -to balance out, compensate for, or even neutralize a *risk*.

outcome -an event, observation, or circumstance, whether subjective or objective, that occurs as a result of an *action* (or *inaction*). In *Taming CHAOS*, a synonym for *consequence*.

outlier -an event or *outcome* that occurs significantly outside the range of what one might normally expect to occur.

peril -a cause of financial loss, harm or injury resulting in an unfavorable *outcome* that could result from taking a *risk*.

possibility -an *outcome* or observation that could happen as a result of an *action* or failure to act. We use the term *possibility* **before** we make a *decision* or choice (when we don't yet know what will happen). A *possibility* will result in an *outcome* that is expected or unexpected.

premium -a specific amount of money that an individual or business pays to an *insurance* company, on a periodic basis, in exchange for the insurance company's agreement to finance or compensate for financial harm or *losses* that might occur as a result of an unexpected *peril* or cause of *loss* such as a flood, fire, injury, or natural disaster.

probability -the likelihood that an observation or *outcome* might happen.

pure risk -a kind of *risk* that has two possible *outcomes*: an unfavorable financial outcome (*loss*) or no *loss* at all.

quantitative calculations -numbers, mathematical solutions, and statistics used to assist in making *decisions*. This can be a part of Step 3 of the *Decision-Making Process*.

random variable -unrelated, chance events that may or may not occur and have some effect on the *frequency* or *severity* of *outcomes*

ranking -the process of listing possible courses of *action* in order of most desirable to least desirable; Step 4 in the *Decision-Making Process*.

reward -a desired benefit (like money, time, or even a subjective benefit like favorable emotions) that we receive as a consequence of taking a *risk*. In *Taming CHAOS*, a synonym for *gain*.

risk -the *possibility* that something undesirable or unfavorable will happen. In *Taming CHAOS*, a synonym for *uncertainty*.

risk charge -an additional financial allocation added to the actuarially determined and expected financial cost of harm or unfavorable outcome, which is included as a part of the total *premium* an *insurance* company charges to help pay for an *outlier* event.

risk management -a Six-Step Decision-Making Process that people can use to consider the range of *possibilities* and their *probabilities,* so that informed *decisions* or choices can be made when facing *uncertainty* or *risk*. The most important objective of *risk management* is to make certain that all methods of managing *uncertainty*—avoiding risk, controlling risk, and/or financing risk—are considered so that individuals, families, or businesses will be in a position to survive and thrive.

severity -the size or magnitude of an unfavorable *outcome* or *consequence*. The *severity* of possible *consequences* often distorts our perception of the *risks* objectively associated with the event.

speculative risk -a kind of *risk* that might result in *loss, no loss,* or *gain*.

statistics -a quantitative field of study that examines and analyzes past historical events for measurable trends, and uses these trends to make predictions about the *possibilities* and their *probabilities* of future *outcomes*. *Statistics* is a field of study that helps people make *decisions* when facing *risk*.

status quo -the way things are right now, and often, the way they have always been.

subjective risk -*risk* that we perceive to be present based on our feelings, intuition or gut instinct, and past experience.

temptation -an *action* or *outcome* that might seem desirable and rewarding in the short-term, but is actually harmful in the long-term or when the interests of others are taken into account.

uncertainty -the *possibility* that something unfavorable will happen. In *Taming CHAOS*, a synonym for *risk*.

worry value -a unique subjective value associated with *risk* or *uncertainty*. *Worry value* is a consideration unique to each individual, family, or business that is difficult to measure or quantify but that must be considered when making *decisions*. Because *worry value* is unique and distinct to each individual, family or business, the risk management method most often used by decision-makers to reduce or lower worry value is *insurance*, which is consistently viewed as the least cost of risk when choosing to employ risk financing as the method to reduce the cost of a potential catastrophic financial loss.

ABOUT THE AUTHOR

Gary is the founder and Managing Partner of The Miller Financial Group, a 2nd generation business practice owner, of an Independent Property & Casualty Insurance, Financial Services & Risk Management Based Consulting Practice, established in the historic Ft. Washington and Spring House, PA areas, operating 68+ years, providing first class professional insurance solutions, sound financial planning & strong risk management based advice & counsel to its clientele.

Gary started his career in insurance over 35 years ago, joining his father's long standing and successful insurance practice which was founded in 1948, and has continued to serve many households and businesses of Montgomery County.

Growing up as a resident of Upper Dublin Township for over 60 years, Gary & his family has lived in Dresher, PA. Gary is a graduate of West Point, commissioned as a Field Artillery junior officer, having earned his BS in Engineering from the United States Military Academy at West Point, NY, serving over 20 years in military service, both active and reserve, with the US Army. Gary earned his MBA in Risk Management from the Fox School of Business, Temple University; served as an Adjunct Professor within the Department of Risk, Insurance & Actuarial Sciences, which is currently ranked as a leading undergraduate program by US News & World Report. Gary is a current member of the Dean's Council, Fox School, Temple University, and has attained the professional insurance industry designation as a Certified Insurance Counselor, (CIC). Gary has been active with the Pennsylvania Independent Insurance Agents and Brokers Association (IIA&B) out of Harrisburg, PA, a professional insurance trade association for independent agents and brokers, serving as a member of the IIA&B Agents Panel for the past 4 years, providing best practice professional standards to its insurance and risk management membership

Gary is a past recipient of the Upper Dublin Township's Citizen of the Year Medal & current member of the UDHS Athletic Hall of Fame. He has been active in his local parish church and has coached at many levels in football, basketball & baseball in Upper Dublin Township. Gary & his wife, Carol, live in Upper Dublin, raising 3 children, all married, currently with 7 grandchildren.

A free eBook edition is available with the purchase of this book.

To claim your free eBook edition:

1. Download the Shelfie app.
2. Write your name in uppser case in the box.
3. Use the Shelfie app to submit a photo.
4. Download your eBook to any device.

Shelfie

A free eBook edition is available
with the purchase of this print book.

CLEARLY PRINT YOUR NAME ABOVE IN UPPER CASE

Instructions to claim your free eBook edition:
1. Download the Shelfie app for Android or iOS
2. Write your name in **UPPER CASE** above
3. Use the Shelfie app to submit a photo
4. Download your eBook to any device

Print & Digital Together Forever.

Snap a photo

Free eBook

Read anywhere

The Morgan James
Speakers Group

We connect Morgan James published authors with live and online events and audiences whom will benefit from their expertise.

Morgan James makes all of our titles available
through the Library for All Charity Organization.

www.LibraryForAll.org